Europe Cities Sketch Vol.2
Adult Coloring Book

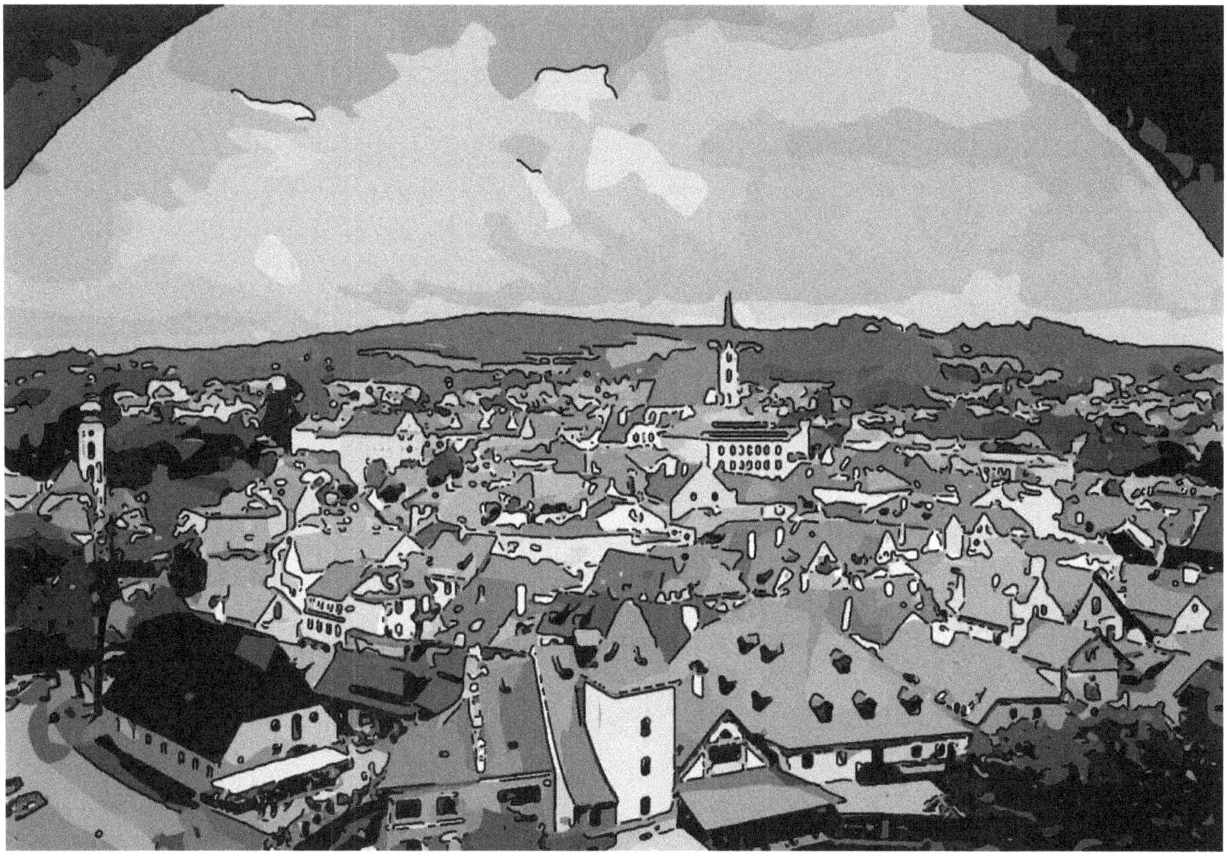

Annie Jr.

Europe Cities Sketch Vol.2 Adult Coloring Book

*Copyright: Published in the United States by Annie Jr.
Published July 2016*

All rights reserved. No part of this publication may be reproduced, stored in retrieval system, copied in any form or by any means, electronic, mechanical, photocopying, recording or otherwise transmitted without written permission from the publisher. Please do not participate in or encourage piracy of this material in any way. You must not circulate this book in any format. Annie Jr. does not control or direct users' actions and is not responsible for the information or content shared, harm and/or actions of the book readers.

ISBN-13:978-1535311397

ISBN-10:1535311398

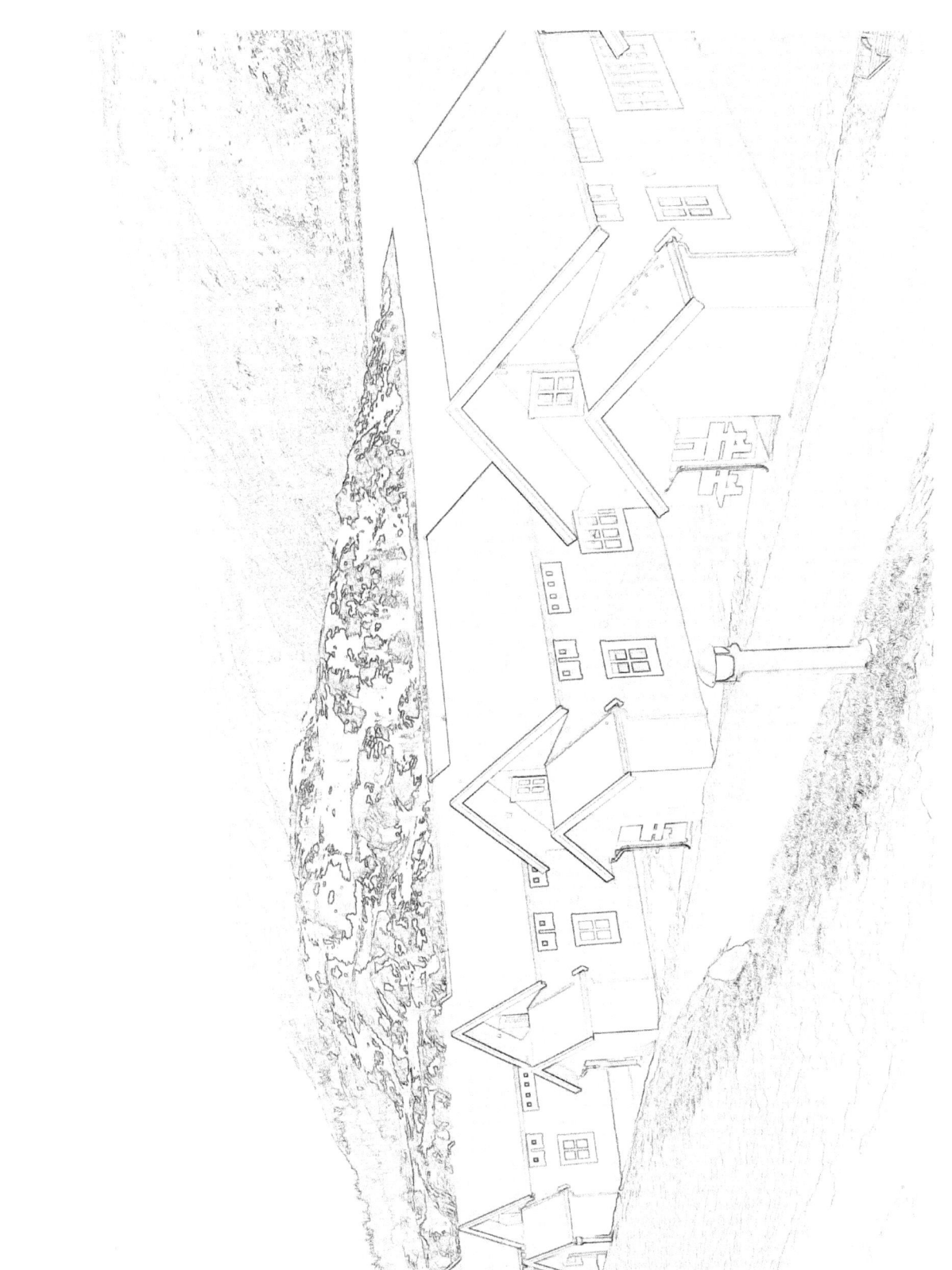

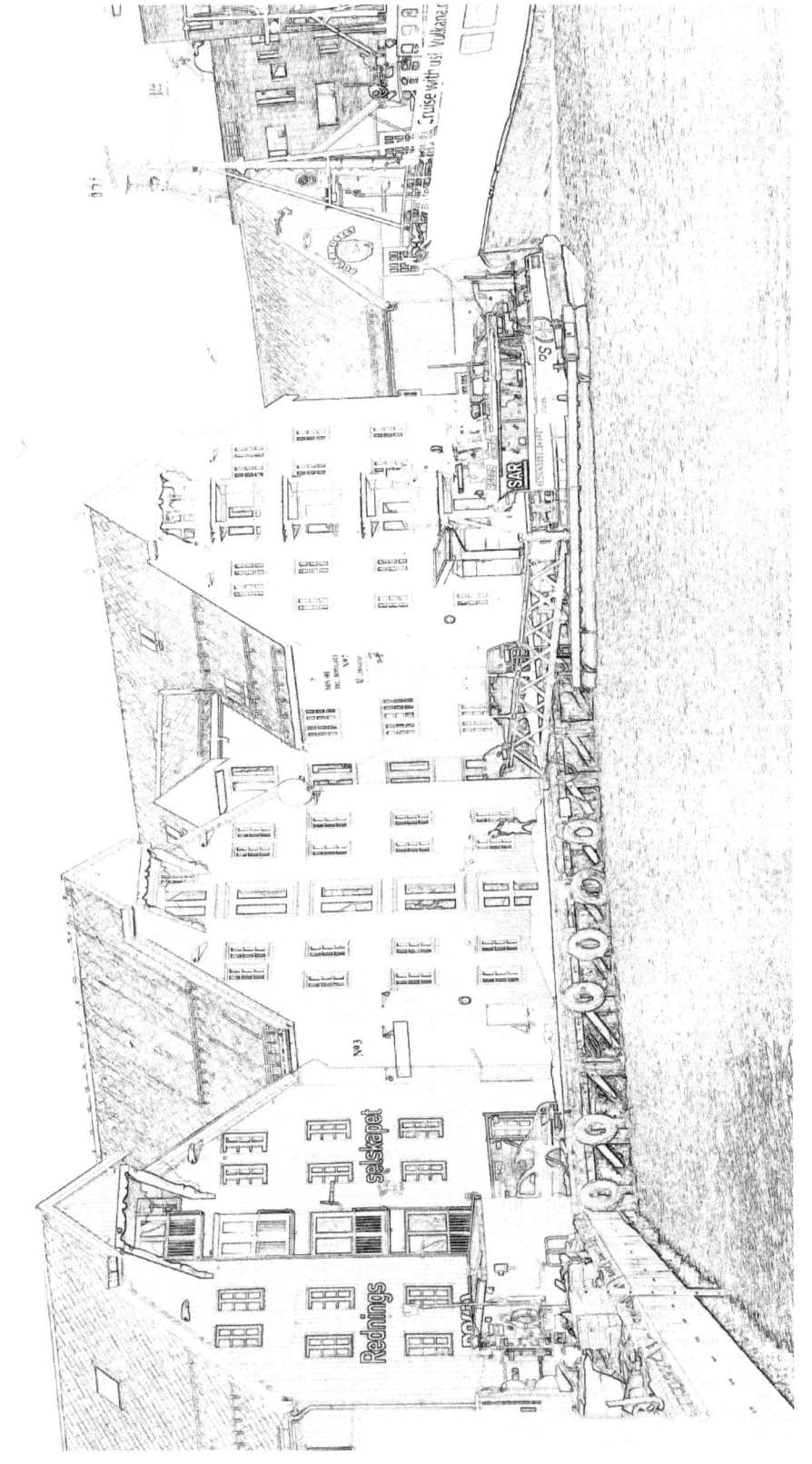

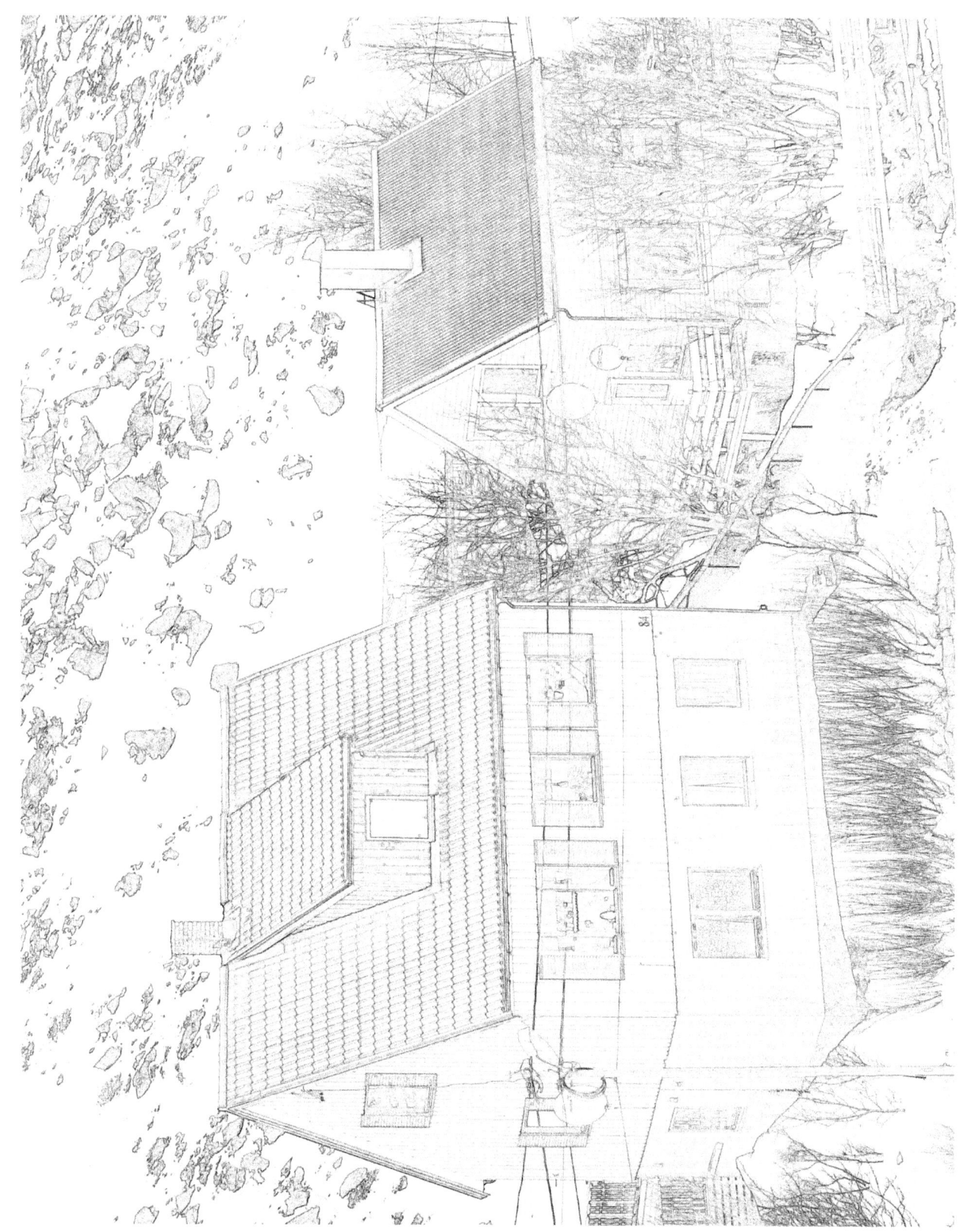

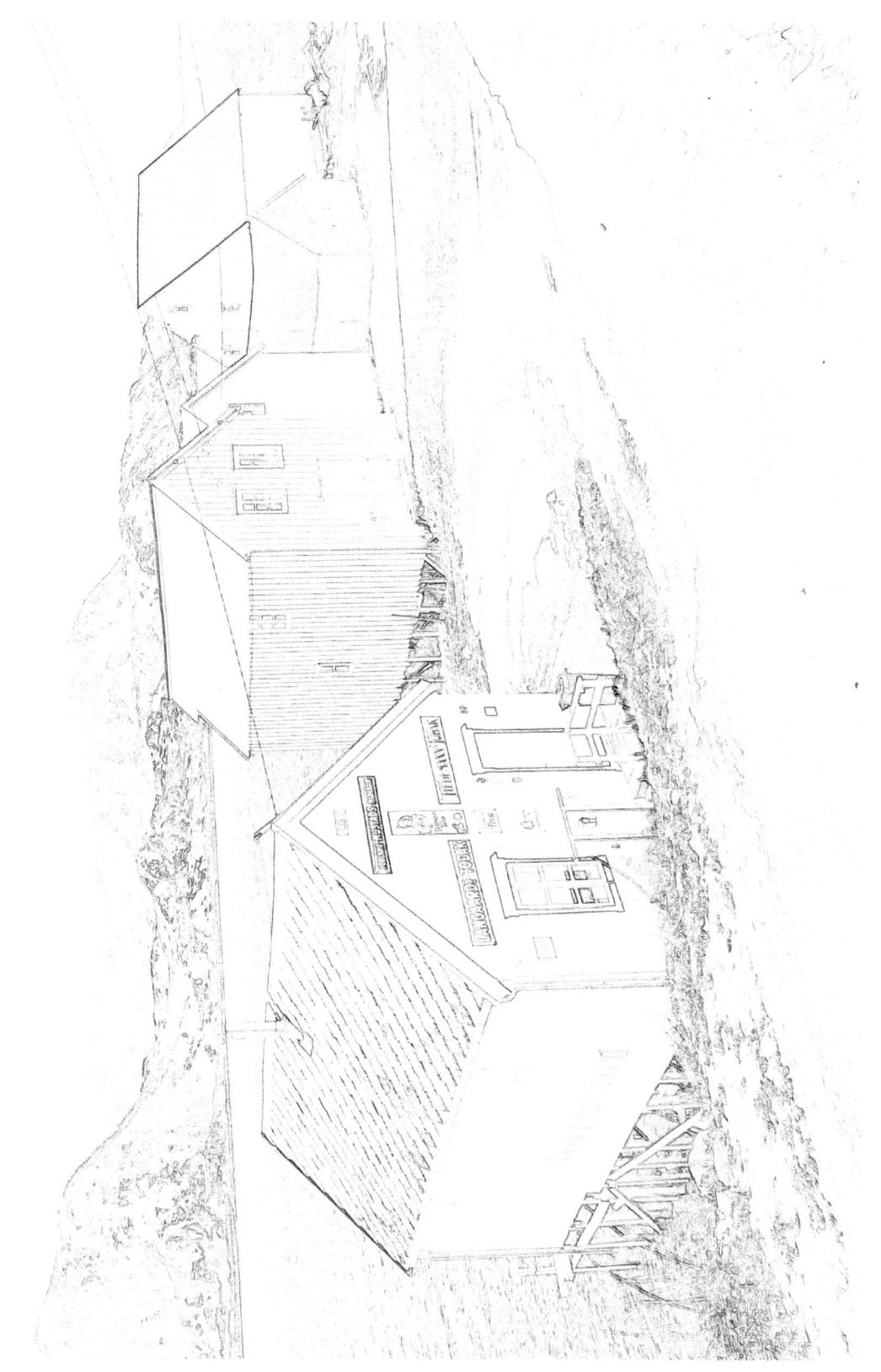

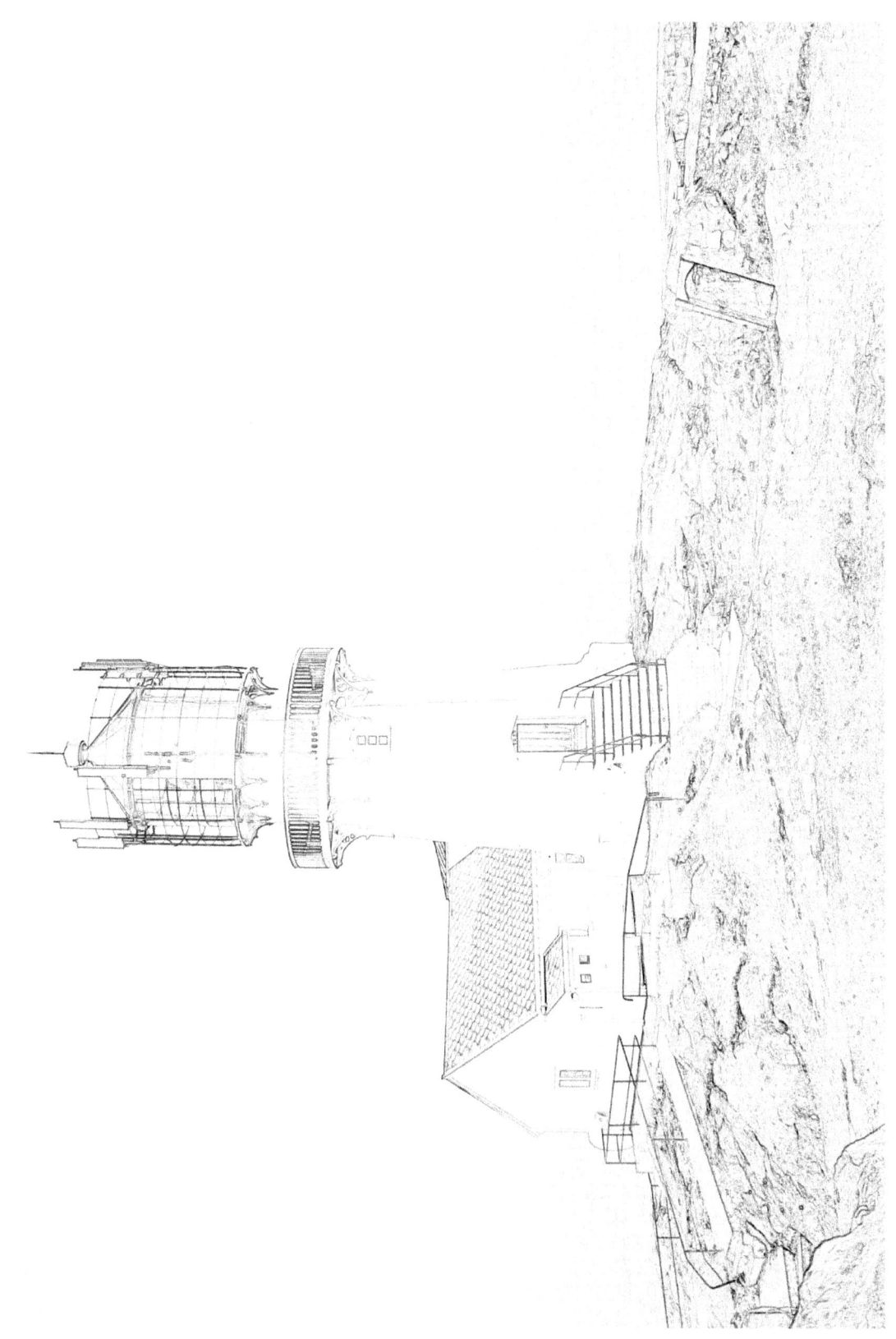

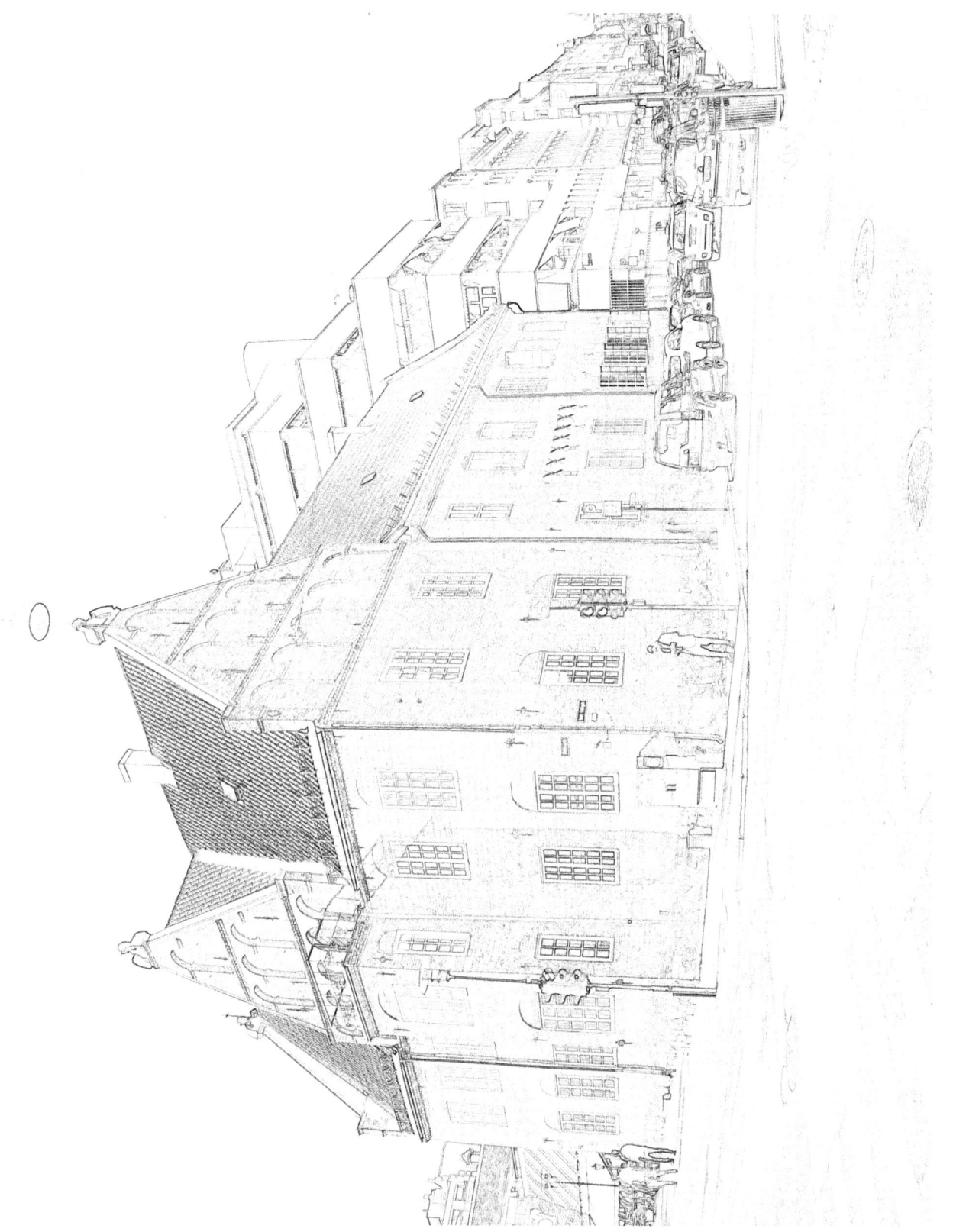

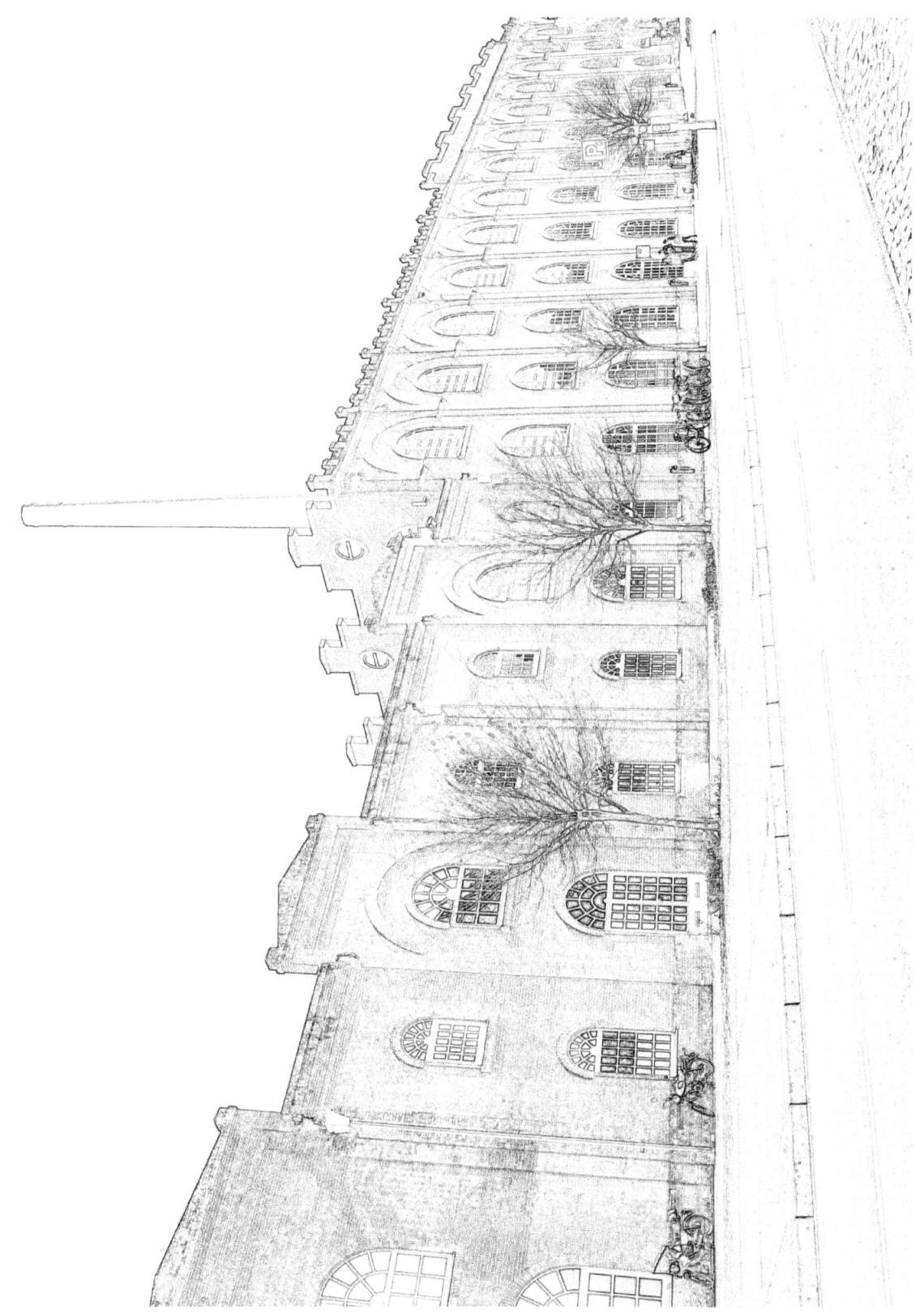

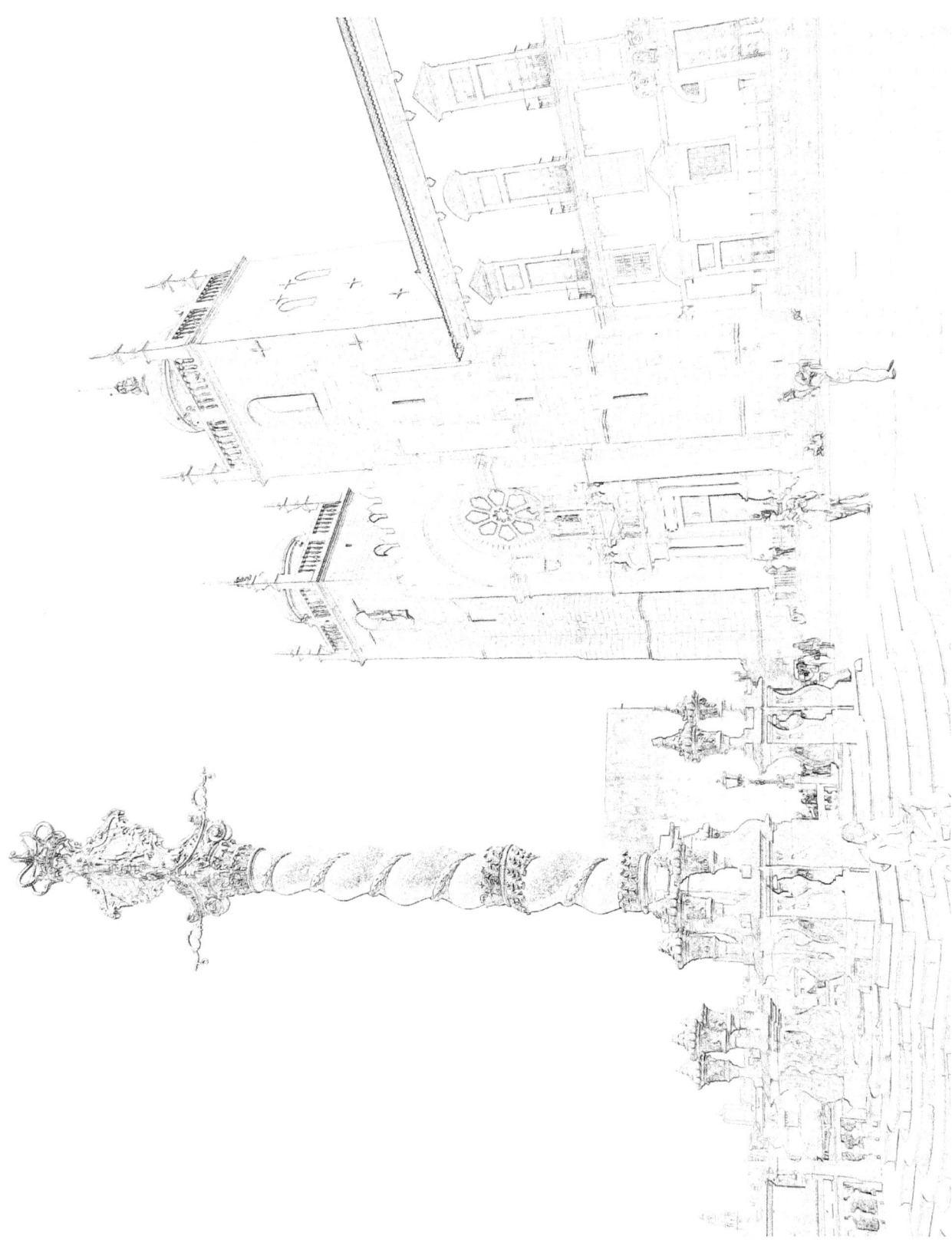

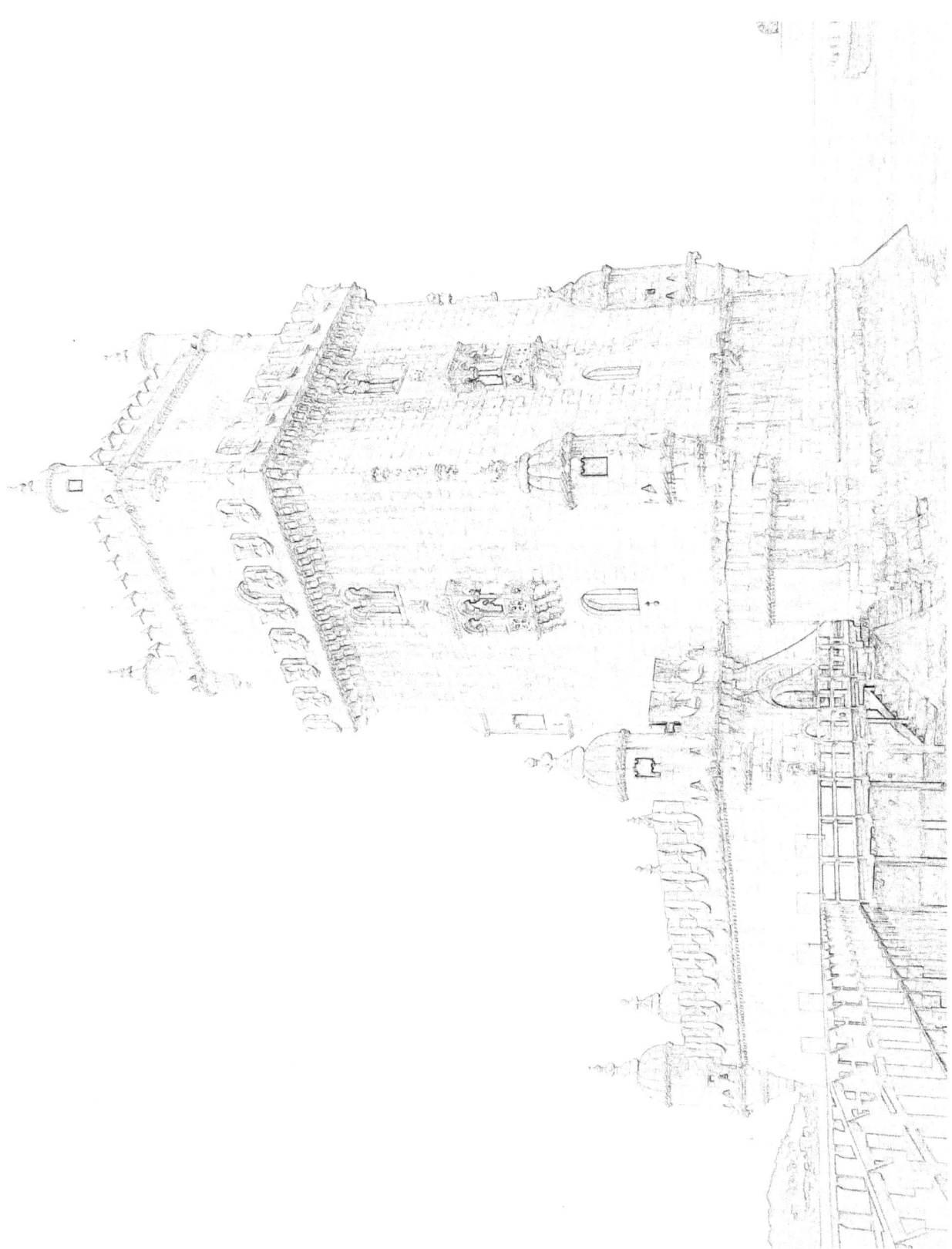

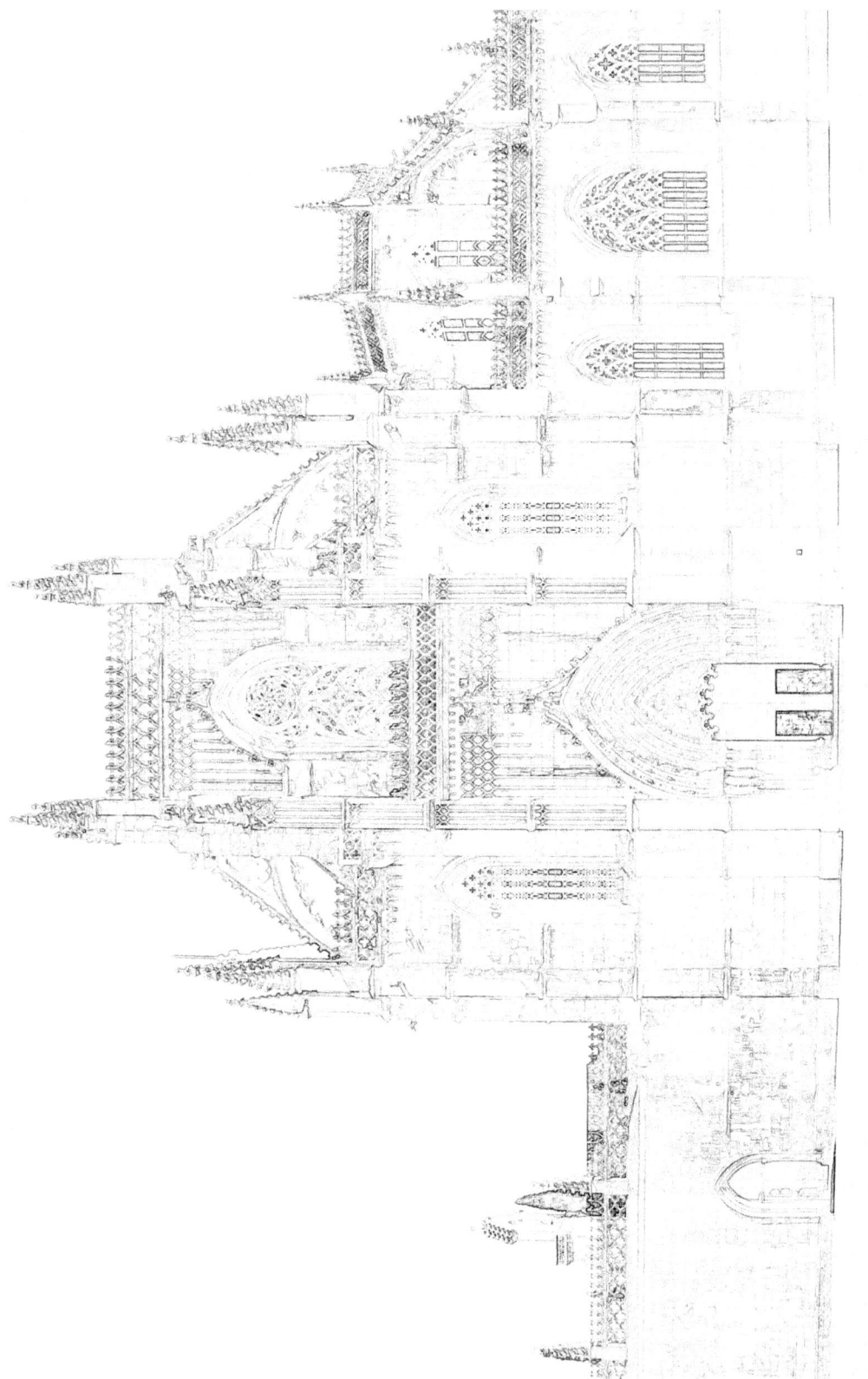

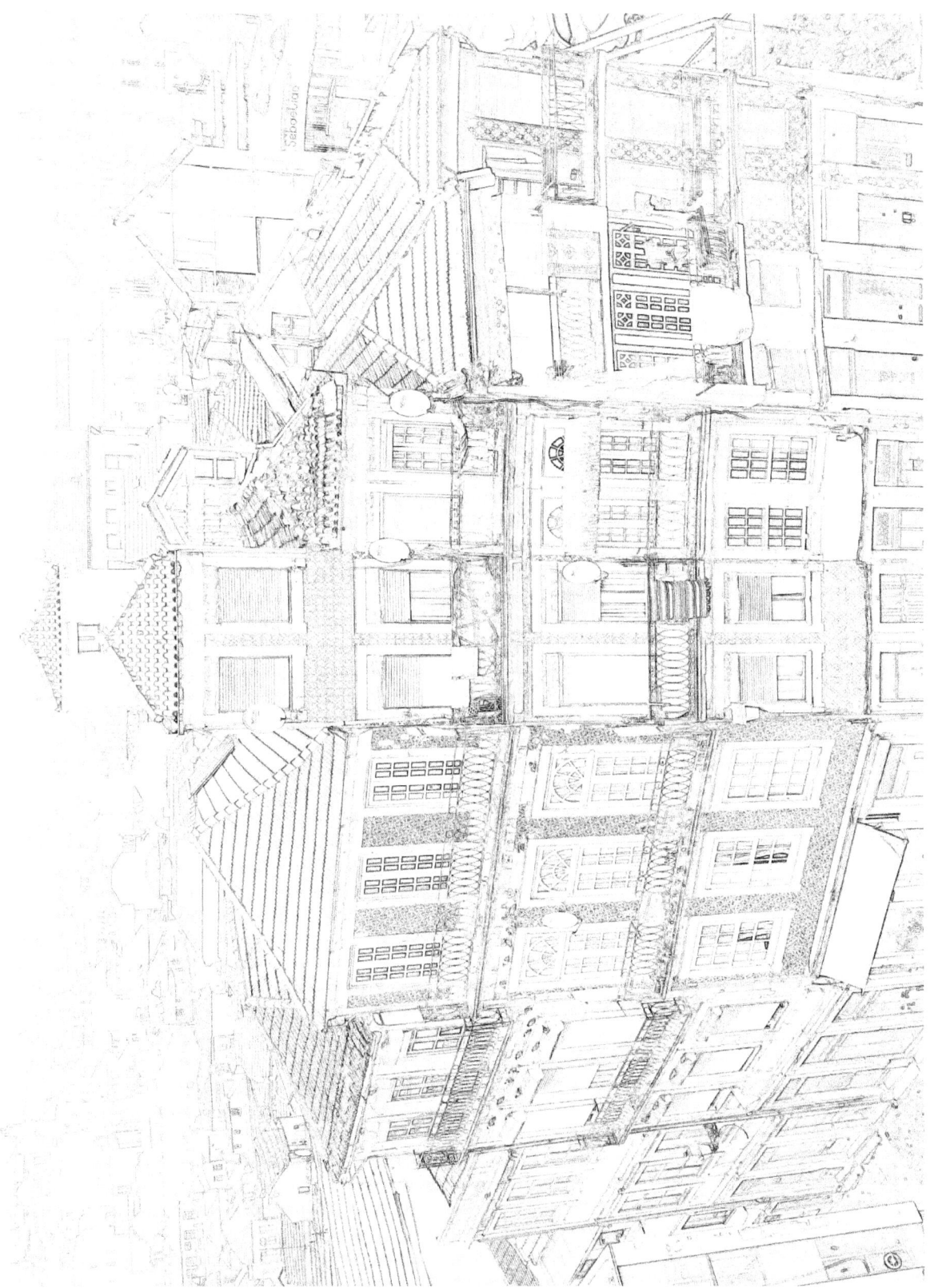

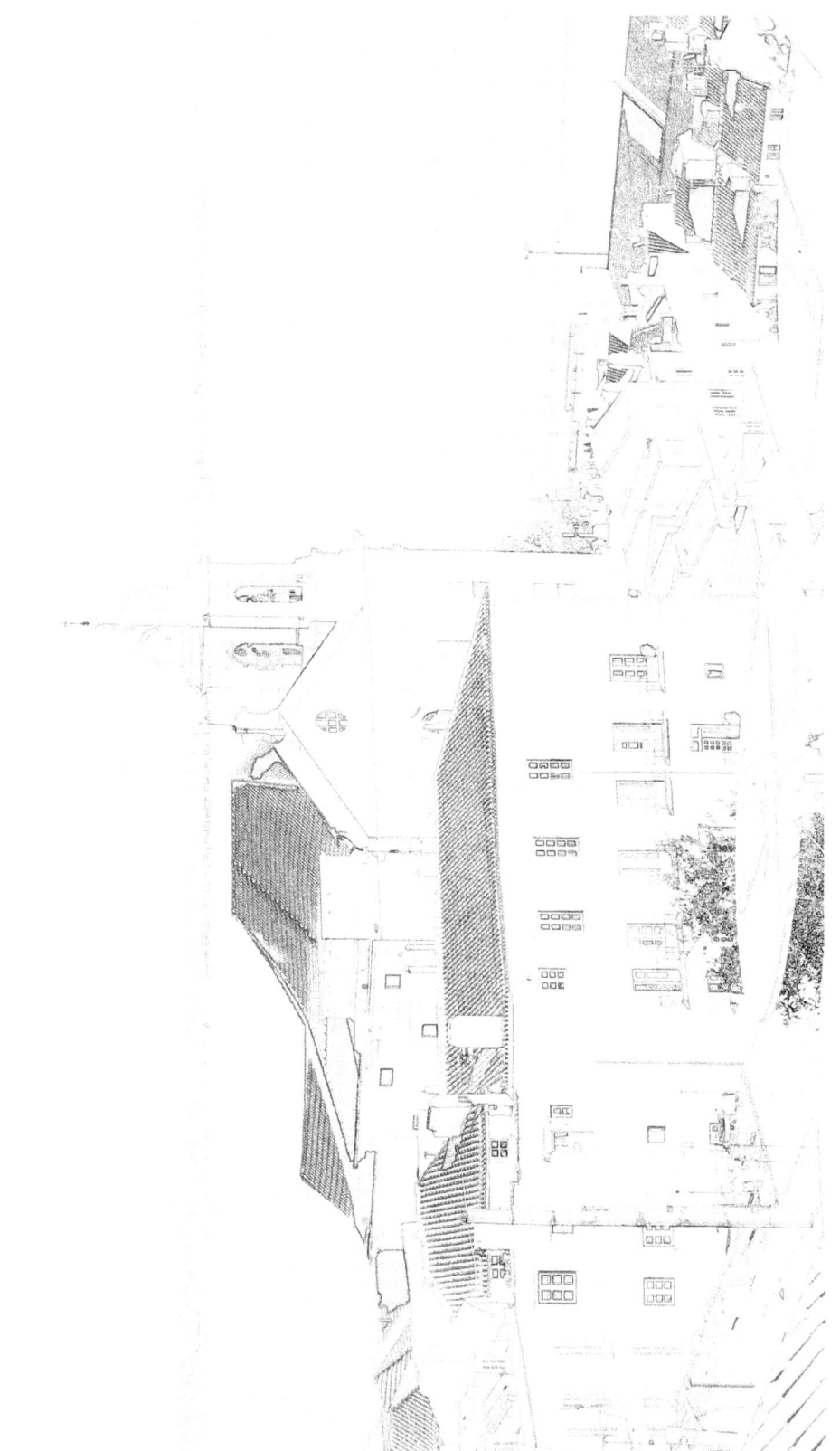

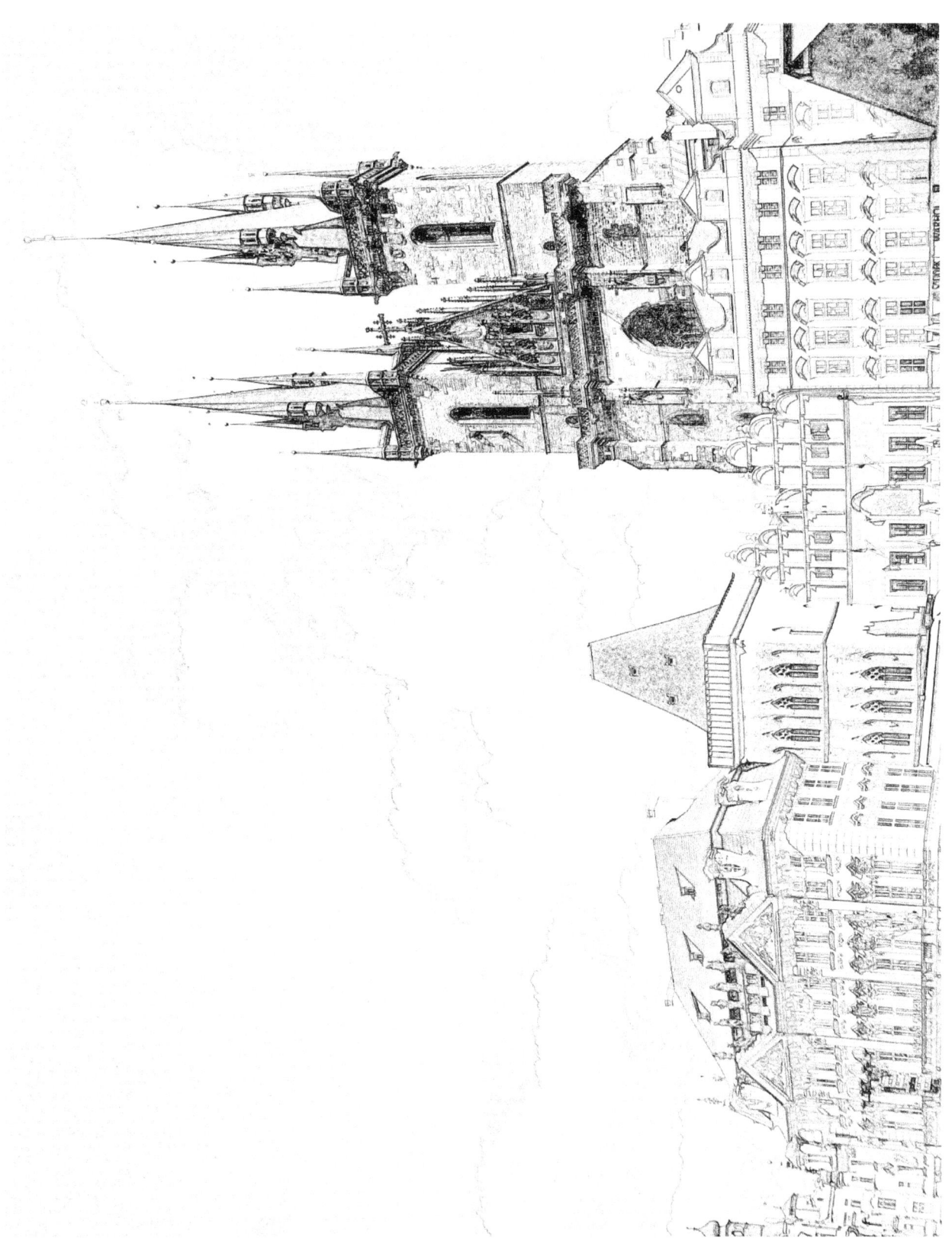

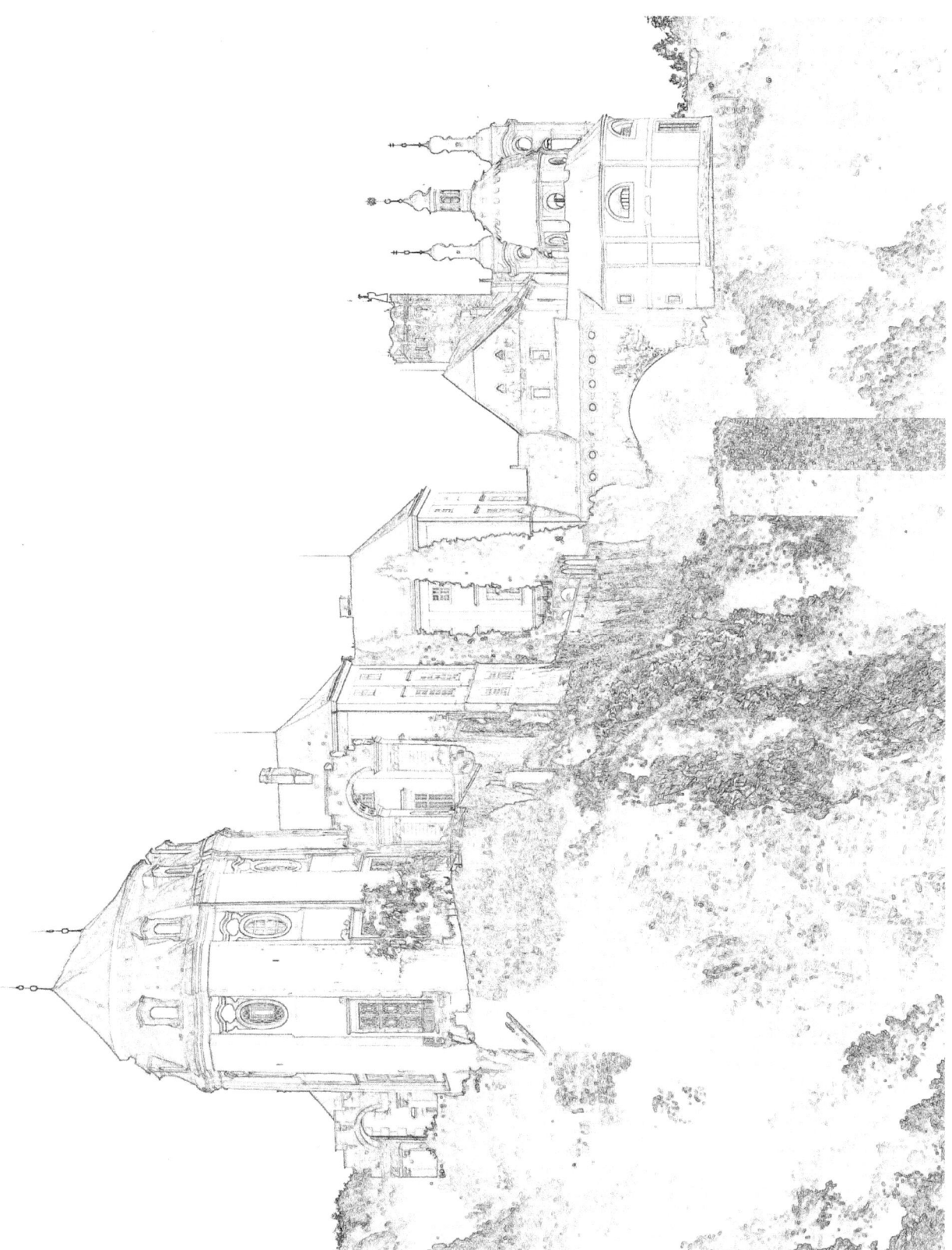

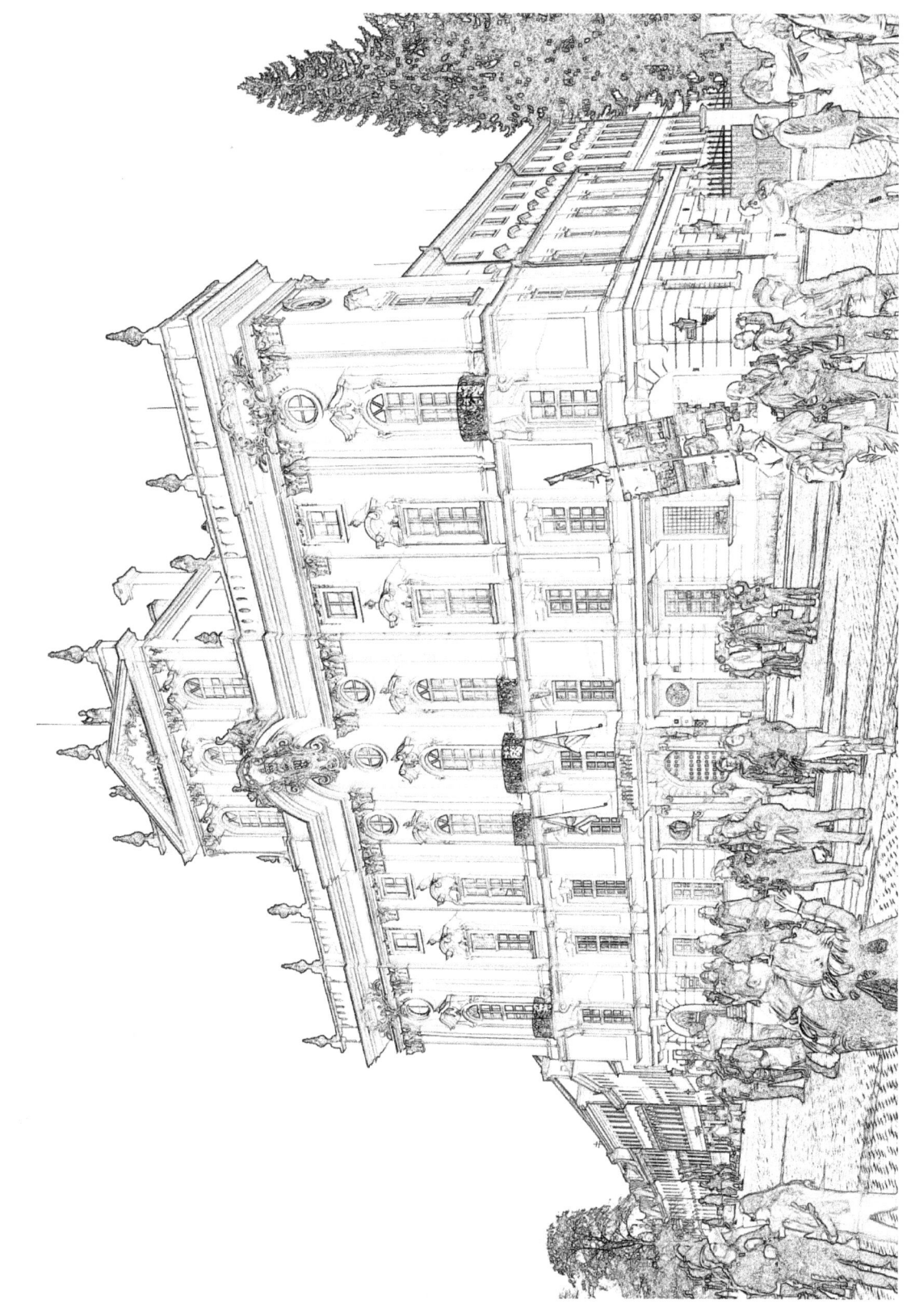

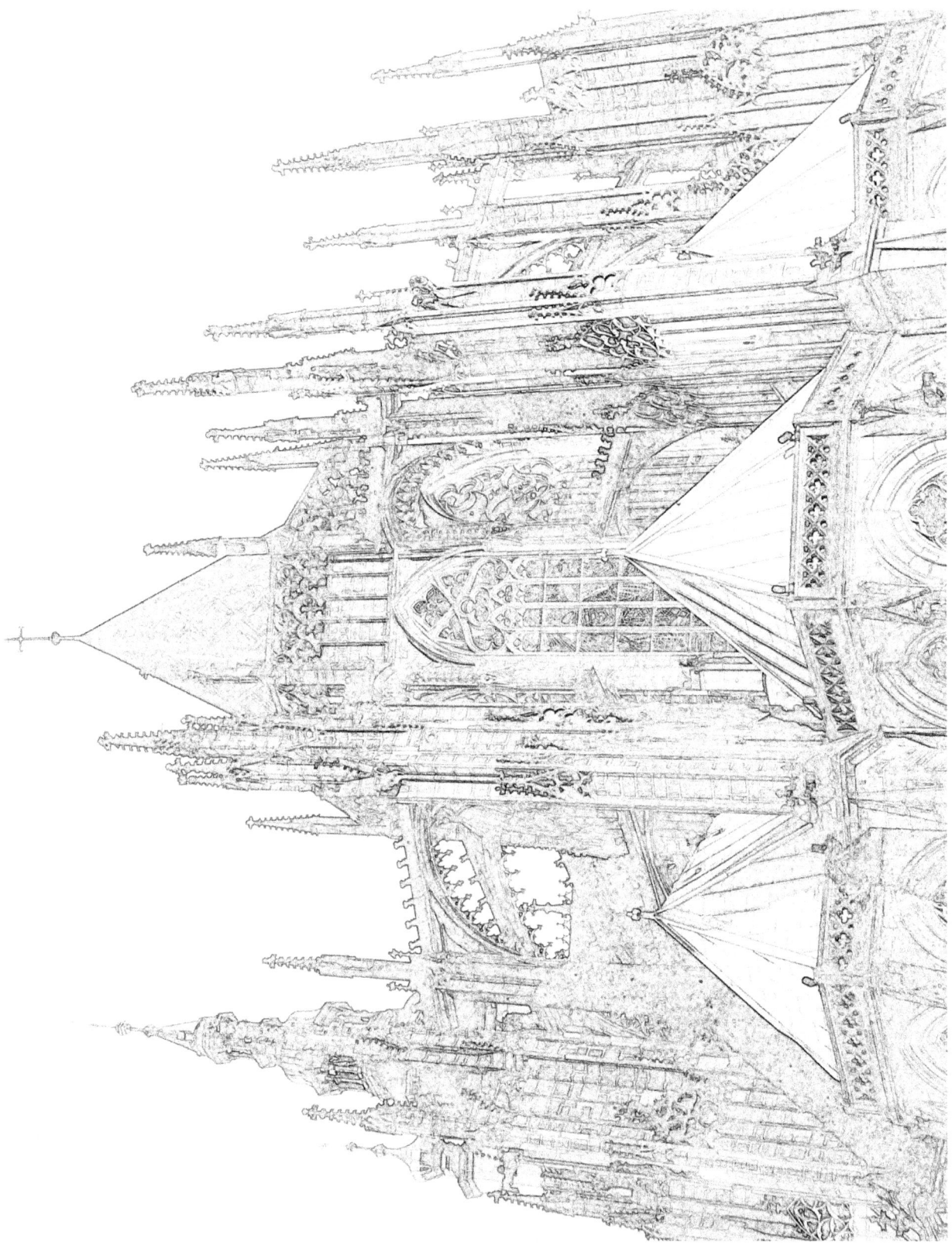

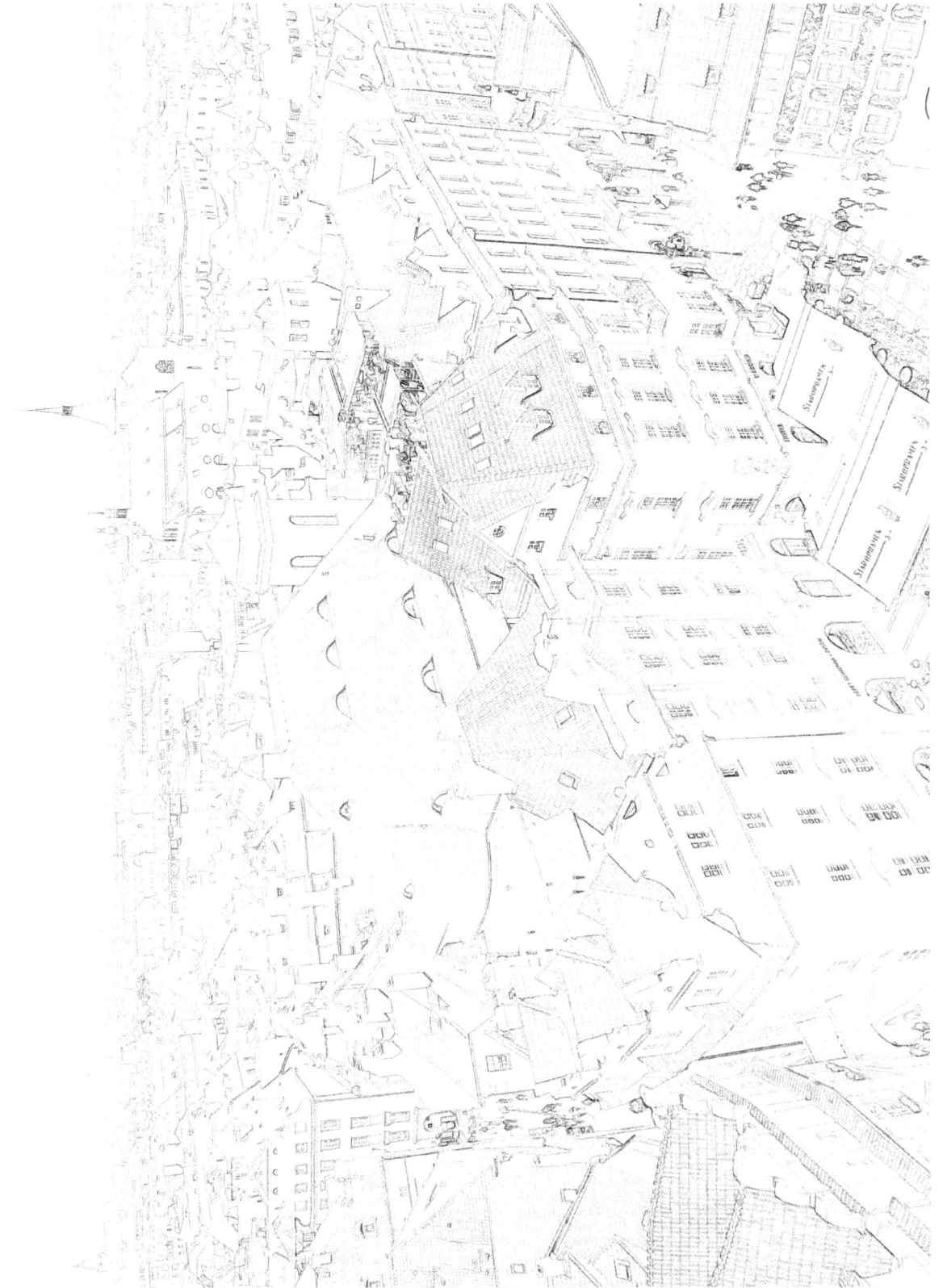

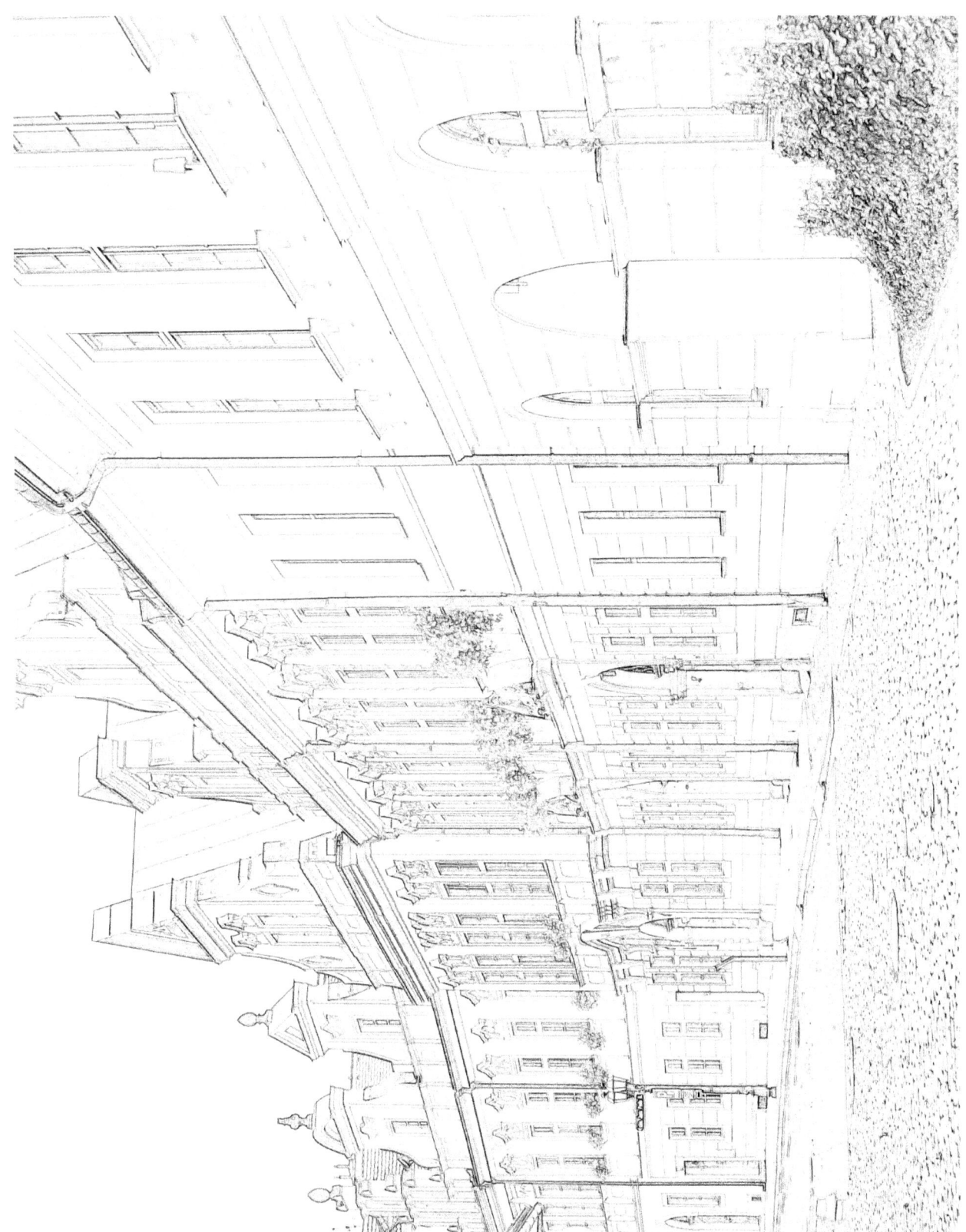

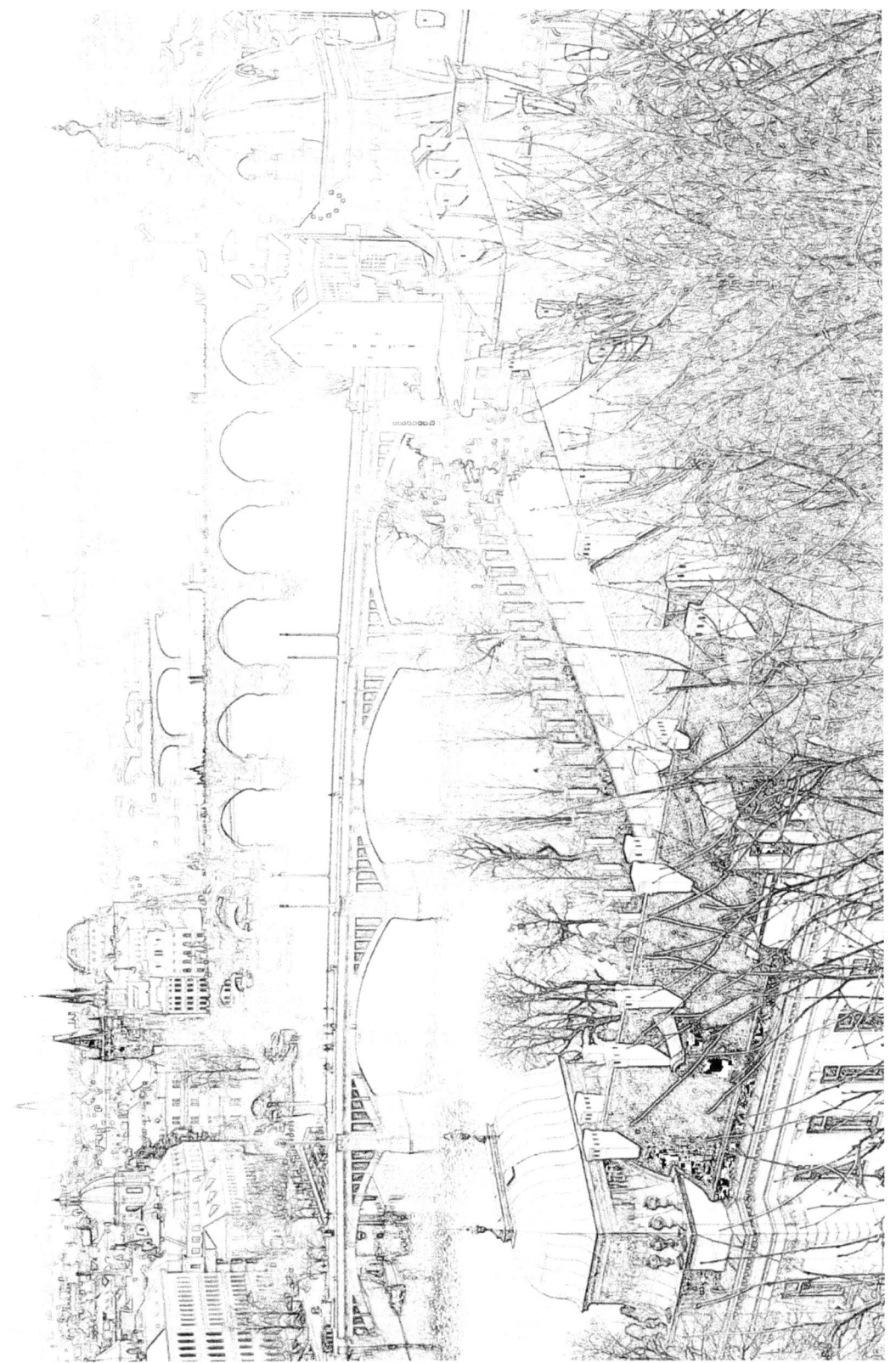

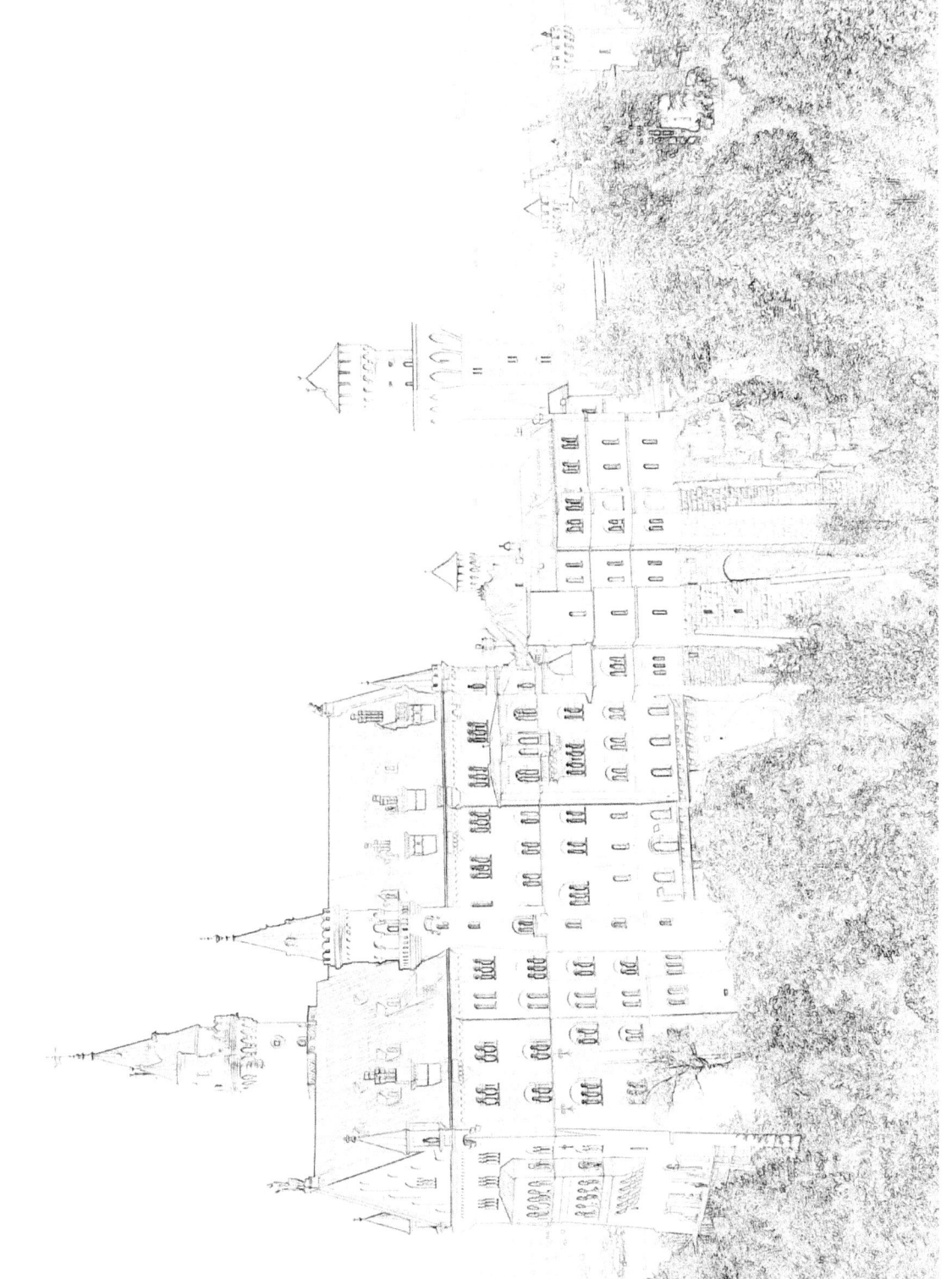

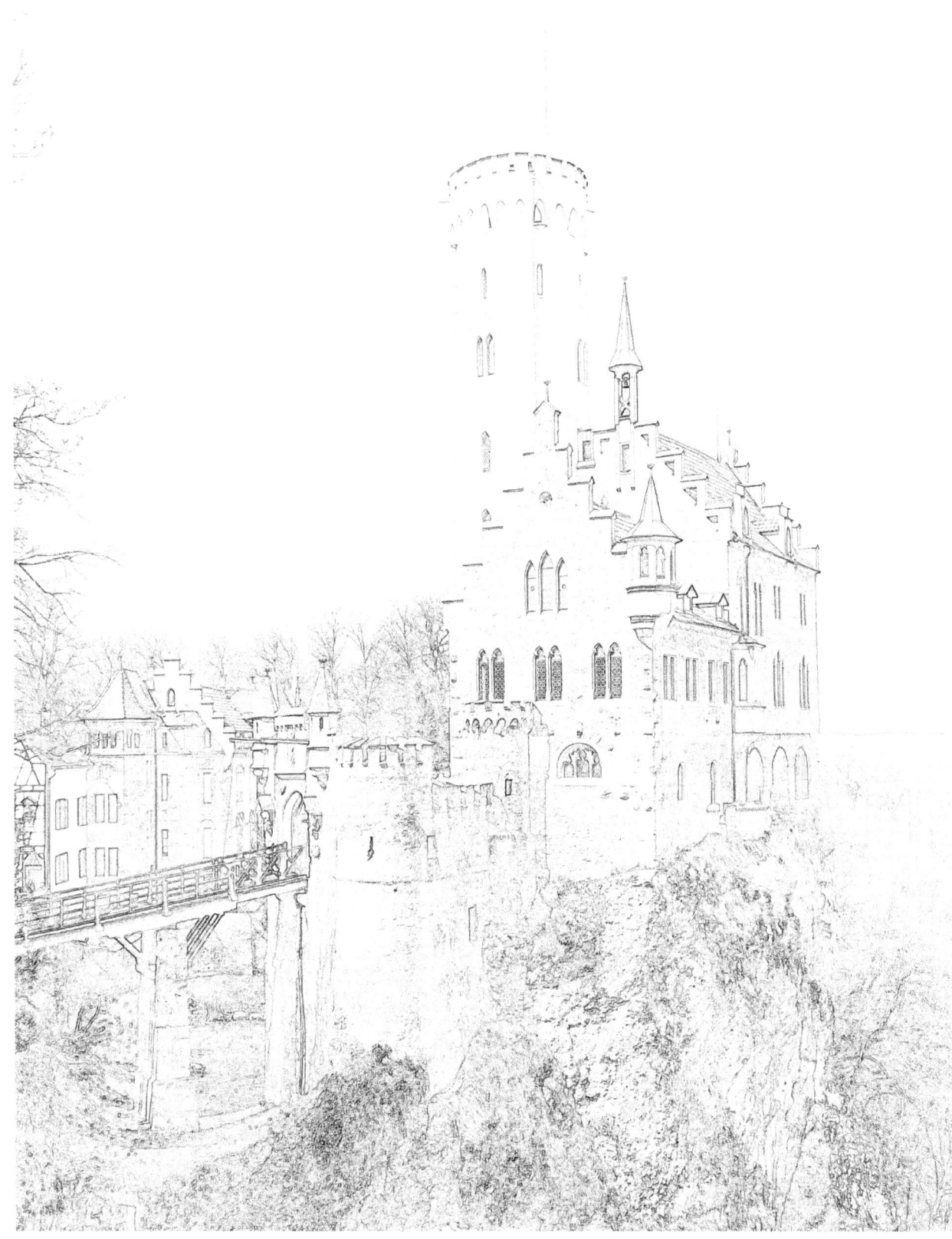

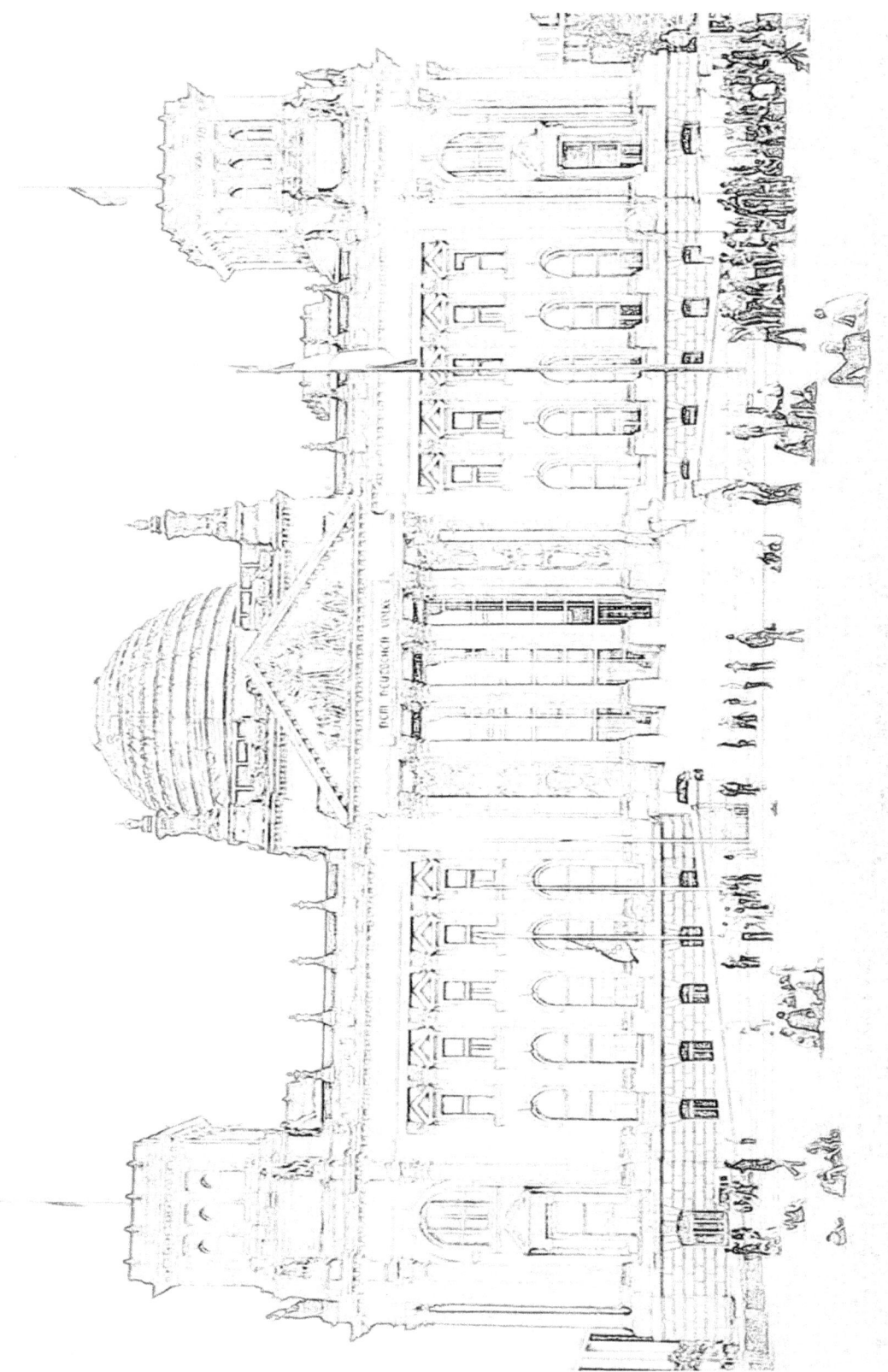

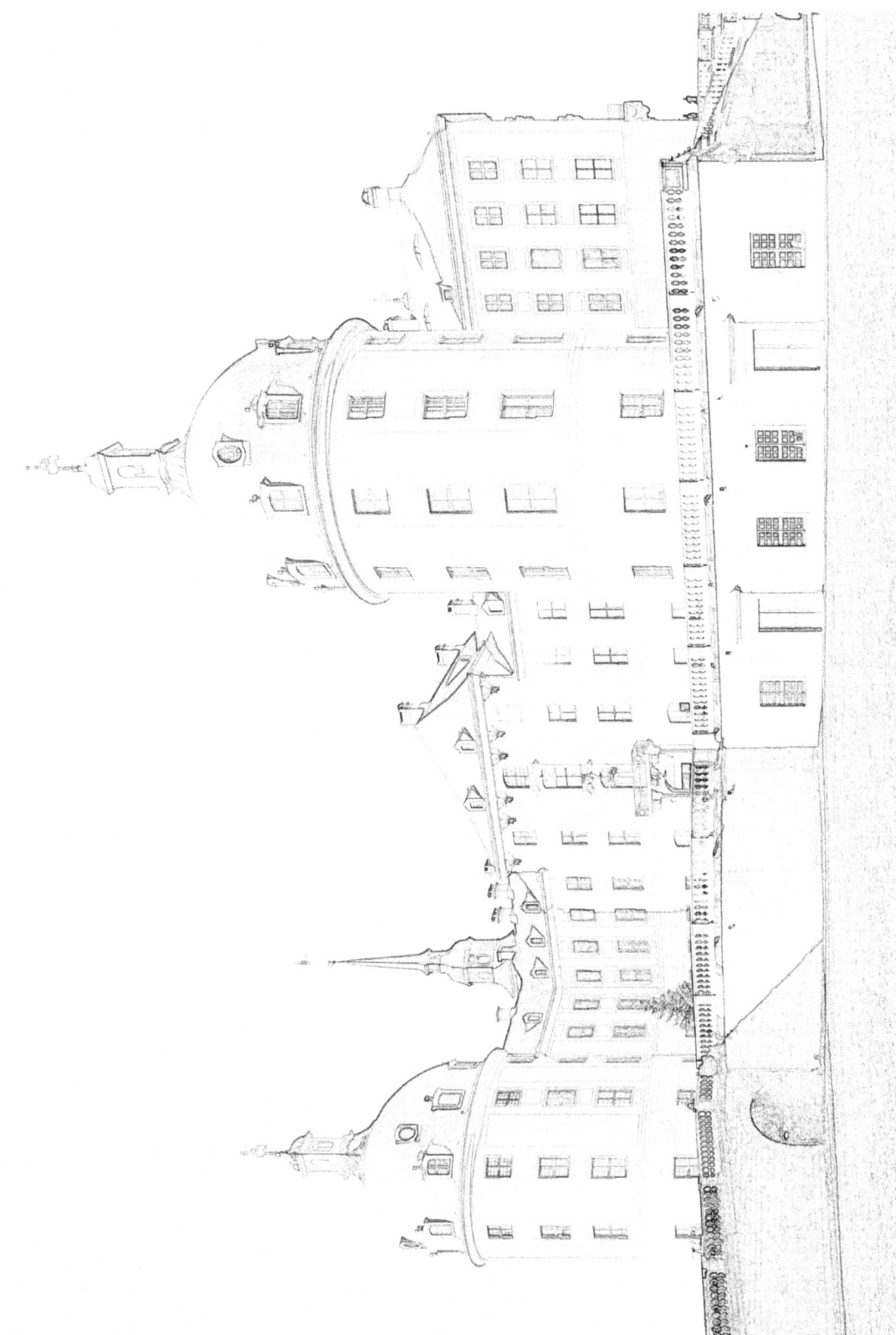

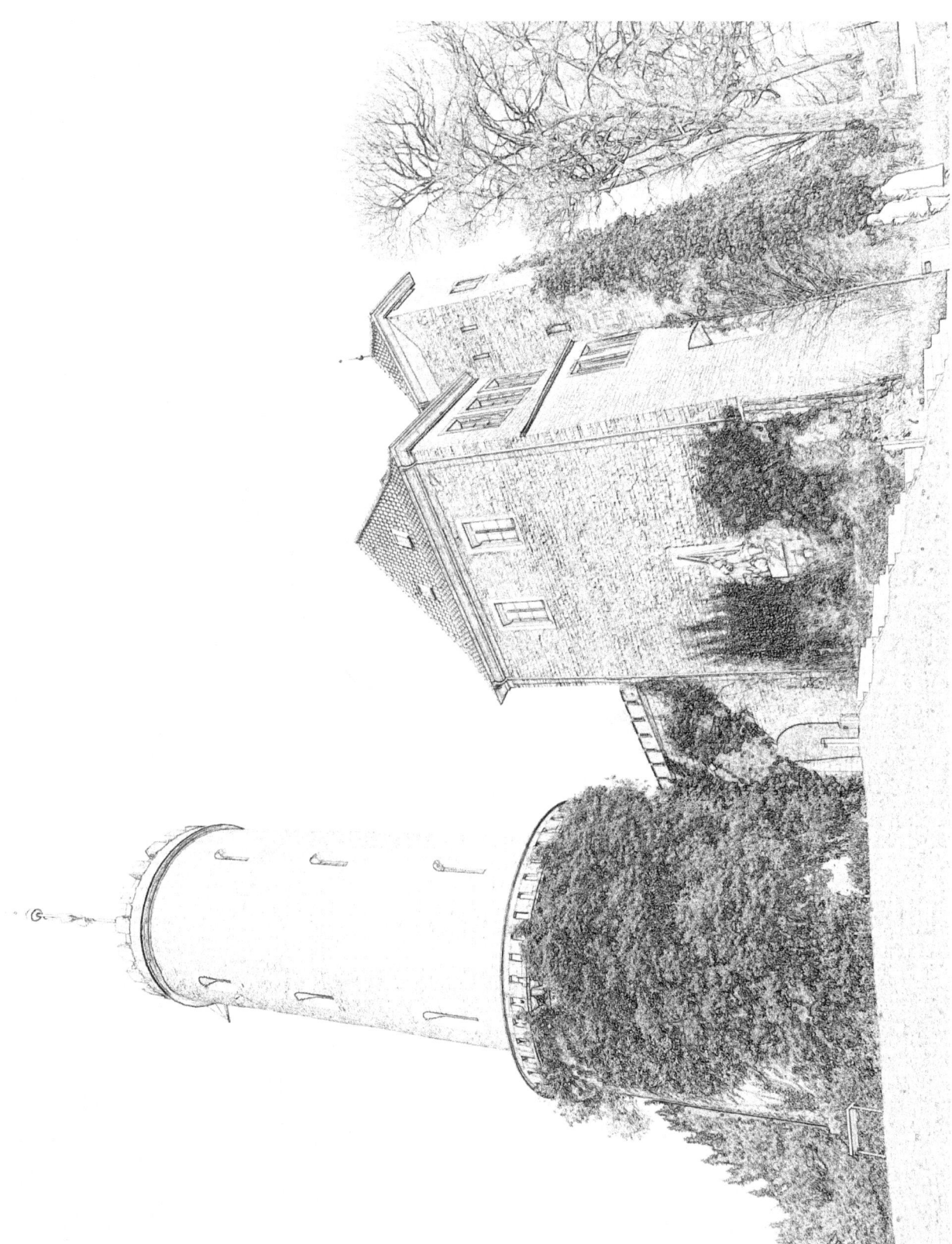

Thank you

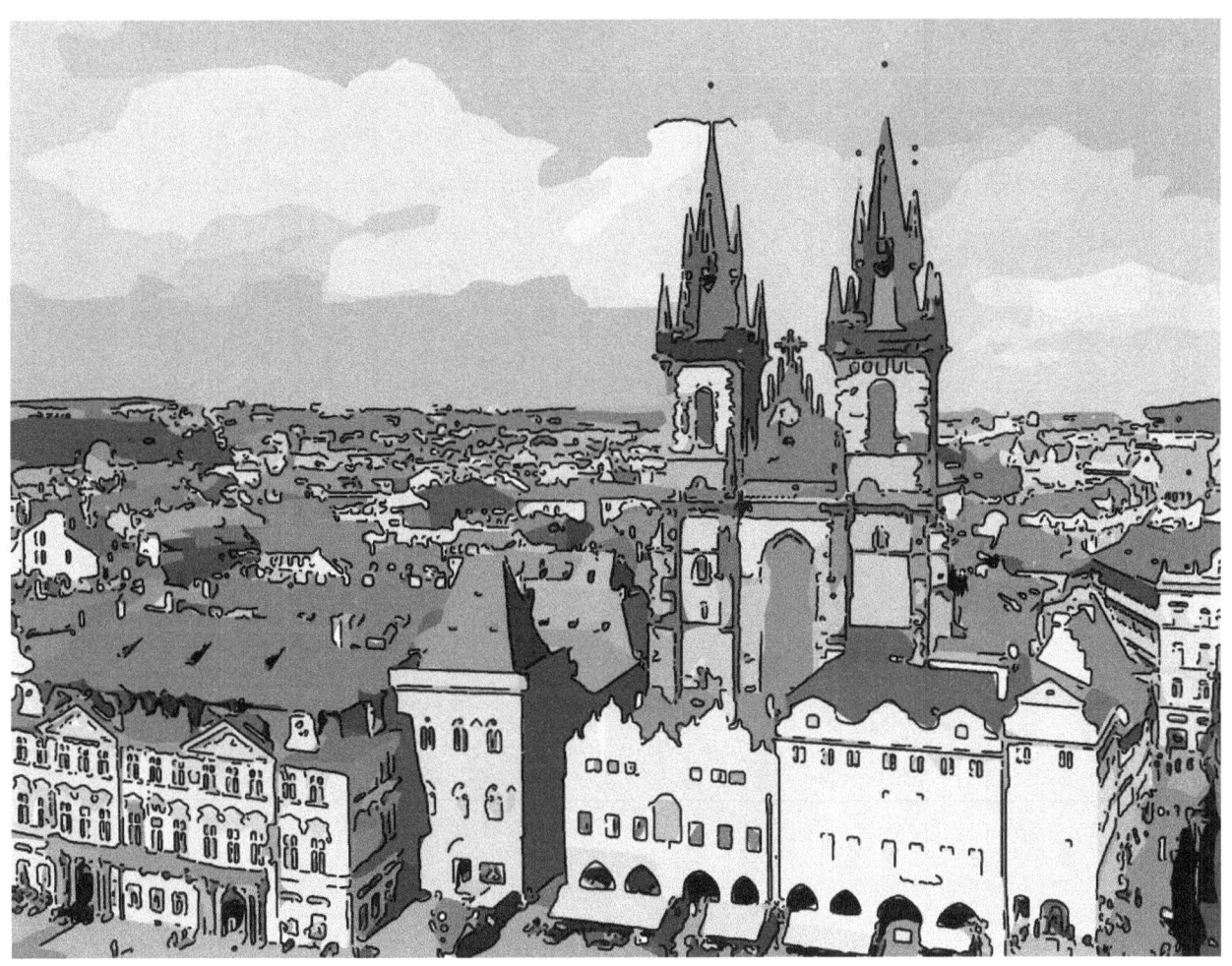